D0371643

Dec. 1988

To my
dear friend
Candy,
Much love always,

Bette

When I Think About You, My Friend

**Dedicated
in loving memory
to Krystyna Maciak**

When I Think About You, My Friend

A collection of poems
Edited by Susan Polis Schutz

Blue Mountain Press ™

Boulder, Colorado

Library of Congress Number: 83-071748
ISBN: 0-88396-196-2

The following works have previously appeared in Blue Mountain Arts
publications:

"Thank You for Being My Friend " and "My Friend," by Susan Polis Schutz.
Copyright © Stephen Schutz and Susan Polis Schutz, 1982. "Special
Friend . . . ," by amanda pierce. Copyright © Blue Mountain Arts, Inc., 1982. "At
the times," "Sometimes I need," and "Being friends," by Jamie Delere; "It is
said," by Andrew Tawney; "Thanks to you . . ." and "Friends," by Lindsay
Newman; "One of the greatest " and "A friend is," by Edmund O'Neill; and
"People like you . . . ," by Laine Parsons. Copyright © Blue Mountain Arts, Inc.,
1983. All rights reserved.

Thanks to the Blue Mountain Arts creative staff.

ACKNOWLEDGMENTS appear on page 92.

Manufactured in the United States of America
First Printing: September, 1983

Blue Mountain Press INC.

P.O. Box 4549, Boulder, Colorado 80306

CONTENTS

We have formed
a friendship
that has become
invaluable to me
We discuss our goals
and plan our future
We express our fears
and talk about our dreams
We can be very serious
or we can just have fun
We understand each other's lives
and try to encourage each other
in all that we do
We have formed
a friendship
that makes our lives
so much
nicer

— Susan Polis Schutz

We meet many people in this life as we go through it. Some will fill minutes, others hours and some, a year or two. And then there are a precious few who touch a place within, and whom we know deep inside that we'll meet again and again.

You are one of these special people to me.

— Linda Gatto

Being friends
with you
is a
very
nice
thing
to
be.

— Jamie Delere

Special Friend . . .

Today, I wish for you all of
the happiness that you are so
deserving of.
I wish that all of your dreams
will be fulfilled
and that sunshine and laughter
will follow you wherever
you go.
I wish you all smiles,
new adventures,
new friends,
and success in everything you do.
I wish you the best of everything
to match the best in you.
And one more wish I have,
more for me than for you,
I wish I could be there with you,
special friend,
to see all of these wishes
come true.

— amanda pierce

One of the greatest joys in my life
is our friendship. I don't think
either of us suspected, when we first
met, that we would stand where we
do today, sharing the close harmony
of our abiding friendship. But we
grew together through the days,
sharing laughter and tears, thoughts
and silence — all the things that
have become an unforgettable part
of who we are. You have always
encouraged me to share myself fully —
my hopes, my dreams . . .

my secret pains and sadnesses
that I have come to understand
better in the light of your
concerned understanding. I hope
I have reflected back to you, if
only in a small way, something
of the same. No one knows what
path tomorrow will find us walking;
but together or apart, I know
that I've found in you
the lifetime friend I have always
wished for, and that
the years passing will never change,
but only strengthen,
our enduring relationship.

— Edmund O'Neill

It sounds simple
but it means so much to say
    I feel comfortable with you.

I don't have to worry
    about how I look to you
    or sound to you
    or what you're going to think about me
    when I'm not around.

I don't have to rehearse or analyze
our conversations —
    when we talk
    I can relax.

You welcome me as I am.
    I don't need to repress or enhance
    my true personality
    for you to be happy with me. . .

We relate as equals.
   There is no threat
   or competition between us.
   Power is not important.
      Respect is.

I feel comfortable with you.
It sounds simple . . .
   but it means so much.

— Paula Finn

Thank You for Being My Friend

When things are confused
I discuss them with you
until they make sense

When something good happens
you are the first person I tell
so I can share my happiness

When I don't know what to do
    in a situation
I ask your opinion
and weigh it heavily with mine

When I am lonely
I call you
because I never feel
alone with you . . .

When I have a problem
I ask for your help
because your wiseness helps me to solve it

When I want to have fun
I want to be with you
because we have such a great time together

When I want to talk to someone
I always talk to you
because you understand me

When I want the truth about something
I call you
because you are so honest

It is so essential
to have you in my life
Thank you for being
      my friend

— Susan Polis Schutz

Sometimes I need
a friend like you beside me
to help me chase away the feeling
that nobody
is here for me . . .

Thank you,
my wonderful and constant friend,
for letting me know
that somebody
        really does care.

— Jamie Delere

Our Friendship Was Meant to Be

Friendships should be spontaneous,
should grow, should spring up
out of themselves, out of harmony,
out of sympathy, out of an
indescribable recognition
of one another.

If marriages are made in heaven,
so are friendships.

— Edward Chipman Guild

There are people in my life
whom I've become friends with —
    instantly.
Although we had not talked before,
    I knew I could trust
    and believe in them
    from the very start.
These people in my life
whom I call my friends,
    my truest friends,
    those I loved instantly —
        are very few.

Meeting them
    provides one of
    life's most special moments —
    unexpected . . .
        like the moment
        I met you.

— Nancy Kuhlka

It feels good to know
that I can always count
   on you . . .
that when you say something,
   you really mean it —
that when you make a promise,
   I can believe it —
I value your word,
I know I can depend on you,
I will always trust you . . .
and that makes me
   feel good.

— Rick Norman

People like you . . .

I like people who are giving and friendly,
those whose eyes are
as kind as their words.

I like people who are thoughtful,
because the special things they do
help to make me thoughtful, too.

I like people who like people.

I like people who care about children;
and people who aren't too grown-up
to have a little bit of child
inside themselves.

I like people who know that grandparents
(their own and other people's, too)
are some of the most important people
in the world.

I like people who like to be outdoors;
who would enjoy an inexpensive picnic
just as much as an expensive restaurant . . .

I like people who realize
   that we're all in this together . . .
   and that every little bit helps.

I like people who love ice cream,
   hate injustice, and couldn't care less
   about gray skies.

I like people who know where to look
   for the silver lining.

I like people who are serious and steady,
   but who can also be just as crazy as
   I can be.

I like people who love to laugh, but
   aren't afraid to cry; people who know
   that the road can be rough, but aren't
   afraid to try.

When I see these qualities shining in someone,
   I know I have seen one of life's
   most beautiful people.
   It's a feeling that I get
      whenever I see people . . .

            like you.

                              — Laine Parsons

Special people are the most delightful
   of all —
They see rainbows
Where clouds could have gone
And in the darkness
They hold the daylight
To a world where only beauty surrounds.

Special people always sparkle —
They radiate a knowing kind of joy
That sees beyond tomorrow
And heeds to no sorrow.

Special people are always peaceful
   and secure
For their world is only filled with love
That opens every door.

You are special people . . .
   to me.

— Nancy Taylor

It is not good
for a person
to be alone
in the journey
of life.

Everyone should
have a friend.

— J. Cowles

I am so thankful
to God for
giving me such
kind friends
to hold me by the hand
while I am passing
through my life.

— Lydia Maria Child

Thanks to you . . .

You were one of a few people
who believed in me at a time
when I most needed someone
    to believe
When I was feeling lonely and
    rejected,
when I was ready to give up —
you were there to give me
    confidence,
you were there to give me trust
And now, thanks to you . . .
I'm not afraid anymore
    to go after what I want
And I don't feel lonely anymore
because I've got a few
    very beautiful people
in my life, and one of them
    is most definitely you.

— Lindsay Newman

I am so vulnerable when
   I am with you.
You have the ability to strip
   away my defenses
and reveal a person known only
   to you,
and I like to think that I
   occasionally do the same
   for you . . .
that you, like me, don't allow
just anyone to invade such
   a private part of your life.

For when it happens . . .
   when our facades are
      put aside,
   when our true emotions
      are unmasked,
the closeness I experience
   with you overpowers me . . .

I feel so defenseless and
   so compelled
to reach out for something
   to strengthen me again,
   to complete me . . .
and how fortunate I am
to have you so close
that I might be fulfilled with
the purity and goodness that
   is you.
Perhaps that is why I don't mind
being vulnerable with you.

Indeed, I appreciate it.

— Barbara Lemke

I didn't ask for
your time,
your patience,
your concern.
I didn't ask for
your calm words
of wisdom.
But the most beautiful
aspect of our friendship
is that you knew
I needed them
without my asking.
That's why I love you,
my friend.

— Paula Morisey

You have a way of bringing sunshine where there are clouds, and warmth where there is cold.

— Laura Campbell

At the times
I begin to feel
     like I'm a nobody,

     you're wonderfully there
to remind me

     that I'm a somebody.

                    — Jamie Delere

There is something warm
in having a friend like you,
something special. It keeps
me mostly dry when the world
is storming all around, and
sends me flying, bursting with
life when the skies grow clear.
It's so awesome to imagine that
merely the thought of another
can do and mean so much, but
if ever my faith begins to fall,
there you are, making me smile.
I'm so glad God made you, and
more, that He put you close
enough to share with me.

— Rowland R. Hoskins, Jr.

This is the wish of your friend:
that each morning of your life
be bright and joyous,
each noontide peaceful and happy,
and each sunset gloriously hopeful.

— T. London

My friend . . .

You are the rainbow that shines
Through the lonely tears . . .

You are a warm embrace that holds
The pieces of my heart together
When it's breaking.

You are the brilliant sunrise that comes
At the end of the long night of despair.

You are a glorious song that fills
My heart with joy and gladness.

You are a prayer that brings hope
To my being when all else seems lost.

My friend . . .
You are love.

— Sally E. Blackhall

True Friendship Is Like . . .

. . . a well built home

Trust is the foundation on which all friendships are based. If absolute trust is not there, then you have a weak foundation that will crumble and give way under the smallest amount of stress causing the house to buckle and fall.

Sharing is the framework that gives each friendship its form. What is shared and how much is shared of day-to-day living — the walks, the talks, the moments of quiet, the tears, the laughter, the toil, the rewards, the pleasures of art, music and the written work — determine the shape and the size of the friendship . . .

Loving is the bond that holds the friendship together. This love grows out of the foundation and holds the framework together. It is what gives the friendship its value and beauty and makes you always welcome . . .

But, no matter how you perceive it to be, friendship is the greatest gift one can give and receive in return.

Thank you for being my friend and for allowing me to be yours.

— Monette

It is said that
a true friend
is the greatest of blessings;
and I know now
that the saying is true,
for I have been blessed
with a wonderful friend
in you.

— Andrew Tawney

In this life
where there are so many
uncertainties
I feel it necessary
to take time out
to acknowledge the
significant things

like breathing,
like being alive,
like having beautiful
        friends . . .

This is just to say
that I'm grateful
for you

— Sharon T. Salter

You're becoming very special to me.

It all happened so gradually, too.
I couldn't tell you when we crossed
    over the line from being friends
    to being special friends.
But I'm glad we did.

I like being around you.
I like myself when I am with you.
Our relationship is based on mutual interests,
    respect and shared support.
I can always count on you
    to let me know that I'm
    doing a good job of being
    the type of person I want to be.
And I think I give you
    a boost every now and then, too.

I feel very complimented that
someone as great as you
thinks I'm pretty special.

I'm glad you're my friend.

— Maureen Dixon

To be true friends,
you must be
    sure of one another.

— Tolstoy

The confidence of friendship
creates a special air . . .
a place
where secrets can be shared
and deepest thoughts
revealed.
A place where conversation
invites no thought of shyness.
A place where
people needing people
meet to enjoy
the freedom born in
the confidence of friendship . . .
the trust of you and me.

— Pauline Smith

To a Friend

In the darkness,
   you are my light.
In my despair,
   you are my hope.
In my fear,
   you are my strength
   steadying my emotions.
In my wanderings,
   you are my guiding hand.
In my heart,
   you are my love.
In my soul,
   you are my friend.

— Beth Steward

There are moments
when one seems almost
to see the soul
         of one's friend . . .

The people I love best
    . . . show me God somehow.

— Ellen Glasgow

One of the hundreds
    of things
that I love about you
is the way you can lift
    my spirit
and make me laugh
when I didn't think
    I could . . .
with only the touch
    of your hand,
the smile on your face,
and a single kind word
    of reassurance.

— Bill Lawton

There is something special
   about you.
After we have been together,
I go away quietly . . . gently . . .
         somehow changed . . .
A little more at peace with
   myself . . .
Content with the world . . .
And better for having been
   with you.

— Linda DuPuy Moore

Some friendships
change with time
Some friendships
dissolve with time
It doesn't matter
what we do, or
what we are, or
where we live, or
how we think
Our friendship
grows deeper and stronger
with time

— Susan Polis Schutz

The years have passed,
    haven't they . . .
and we have gone through
    the many changes together
    and have grown
closer together than
    I ever even hoped for.
As far as loyalty is concerned,
you have been a priceless example
of what a friend should be,
and our companionship together
has inspired so many moments
    and so many delights.
You have become
my most sincere confidant.
You have listened to my tales,
    my wanderings and my searches,
and have passed from friend and
    companion to so much more . . .
Inside of me there is . . .
and you should not be surprised
    to know it . . .

            a wonderful love for you.

                    — jonivan

"Special" is a word
that is used to describe
something one-of-a-kind
like a hug
or a sunset
or a person who spreads love
with a smile or kind gesture.
"Special" describes people
who act from the heart
and keep in mind the hearts of others.
"Special" applies to something
that is admired and precious
and which can never be replaced.
"Special" is the word that best
describes you.

— Teri Fernandez

You can depend on me

Friendship is
for serene days
and graceful gifts
and country rambles;
but also for rough roads
and hard times.

— Emerson

When someone believes in you
it is easier to
    believe in yourself.
To know that
    someone will remember
      your star
when everyone else has forgotten
    it was ever shining at all
    keeps you looking to the sky.

It is good and strong
to be happy for yourself and
    all that you do . . .
It's just that when
    someone like you
      has faith in
    someone like me,
      the happiness is
        easier to find.

— Laura West

I've had many friends
but few have strived to fill
the silent needs,
    the untouched corners
You are an original among
    those few
You set an open example
    with your love
You give with your life
and listen with your
    sensitivity
You care enough to be
    the best you can,
and in turn, you bring out
    the best in me.

— Dorie Runyon

You are a free spirit
with an honest heart
and a genuine smile.
That not only makes you
an extraordinary person,
but an extraordinary
friend
as well.

— Sheri Martin

"Being a Friend"

A friend combines three wonderful things;
    love, sympathy and help.
A friend is one who considers a need
    before one's deserving.
A friend is so many things . . .
the jewel that shines brightest in the darkness,
an encourager of the nobler side of our nature,
a star of hope in the clouds of adversity,
a diamond in the ring of acquaintance,
a volume of sympathy bound in love,
one truer to me than I am to myself,
one who understands a silence,
a link of gold in the chain of life,
the essence of pure devotion,
the warmth of sunshine,
a friend . . . like you.

— T. London

Friend, you give me more
in just being my friend
and caring for me
than any fortune on earth . . .
My heart goes out to those
who do not know the treasures
hidden in a smile or
the comfort found in the
        outstretched arms of a friend.
You'd give your life for me
and I mine for you.
And though we're not put to the test
we know,
and it is in the knowing
that we can face each day
with a smile around our hearts.

— Annabelle Armstrong

The greatest of delights
and the best of joys
is to know that
   people like to
   be with you,
and to know that
   you like to be
   close to them.

— Maxim Gorky

A friend is a dream
of all the best life can offer —
a generous and caring heart
that outshines all distances
and times between two people;
a companion in all
the stormy and sun-filled times
life passes through;
a unique warmth and joy
from the knowledge that
a special person exists
who always believes in the best
and for the best;
and an infinite number
of things, spoken and unspoken,
that create and make strong
the bonds of friendship.

And you, my friend, are a dream
that makes my life
one of the very best.

— Edmund O'Neill

my dear friend,
you must **feel** how I thank you,
for I cannot easily say it.
I have come to realize
how special everything is
that you have given me . . .
　　both outwardly and inwardly . . .
and always, given warmly,
in your own wonderful way.

— Cassie O'Neal

Thank you, friend

It is with as much gratitude
    as ever a heart felt,
that I sit down to thank you,
my dear friends . . .
for the continuance of your
    attention to me . . .
I can never thank you enough,
and yet I thank you from my
    soul —
for the single day's happiness
    your goodness sent to me,
I wish I could send you back
    thousands —
I cannot, but they will come
    of themselves —
and so, God bless you.

— Laurence Sterne

Who, but a friend . . .
   can sense your voice before
    you call
   and feel your need to talk
    before you speak

Who, but a friend . . .
   gives of themselves and in
    return seeks only the warmth
   of your presence and the
    happiness of your smile

Who, but a friend . . .
   shares our dreams, our tears
    and our blessings
   and asks only for love in return . . .

Who, but a friend . . .
   has the power to spread their
    love across many miles,
   to bring kindred souls together
    with their magnificent charm

Who else, but you . . .

— Edith Schaffer Lederberg

Stranger —

That is what you were to me
And I to you
Not long ago.
Friend —
That is what you became
The moment we met
Not long ago.
Whether it was fate,
Or luck or chance,
All I know
Is what there is to know —
Our paths crossed once
And that is all it took
Of the millions of people
In this world,
We met
And little did we know
That our slight meeting
Was the beginning
Of a lifetime friendship.

— Lois Reiko Shikuma

If each of us
is fortunate,
we will have a few friends
   in this world
whose belief in us is strong
whose love for us is true.
Please . . .
   when you think of those
who care for you,
who wish only the best
   for everything you do,
be sure to remember my name
as one who believes
in you.

— T. London

there are some people
to whom you can say "hello"
and get a cherished smile

there are some people
with whom you can talk
and get laughter rich and free

and then
there are special ones
with whom you can cry

it pleases me, my friend,
that you are all three

— Sharon T. Salter

With You in My World . . .

My eyes feel the deep peace
of the sky,
and there stirs through me
what a tree feels when
it holds out its leaves
like cups to be filled
with sunshine.

— Rabindranath Tagore

You've been more to me than a friend . . .
We've shared more than most people do —
   feelings that time won't erase
No words can ever let you know
   the peace I feel when you are near
In times of trouble, your eyes express
   exactly what I need to hear
In times of joy, your smile says
   you're sharing what I feel
In times of doubt, I always knew
   I could trust in your loyalty
We've stood the test across the miles
   And watched our friendship grow
I've come to learn, when it comes to friends,
   there's no one quite like you.

— Marie Grady Palcic

If I could reach up
and hold a star
for each time
you've made me smile,
an entire evening's sky
would be in
the palm of my hand.

— Rowland R. Hoskins, Jr.

Sometimes, I can't believe that
    we've remained friends
through all the changes we've
    both seen.
But I'm glad that we survived them,
and I think we can survive anything
    else that comes our way,
and I just wanted to say ``thanks''
    for the memories.

— Rick Norman

We were friends
when we attended school together
since then
we have followed different paths
living in different places
We grew apart
yet we grew together
Our years of sharing
and discussing
every thought, every idea
and every experience
led us to know each other
so very well
No new friend could ever understand
us as we understand each other
Though we don't see each other
as often as we used to
our friendship still
grows stronger
every day

— Susan Polis Schutz

I would rather have
a friend
than a painting
or a poem
or a song . . .
For a friend
is all of these,
and so much more.

— Beth Garry

Together, we've weathered
    the toughest of times,
comforted one another,
    when comforting was needed;
spoken words of assurance
    when one of us was feeling
    insecure;
dried each other's tears
    when our emotions got the
    best of us;
and felt love in the silence
    we shared when no words
    seemed appropriate . . .

Together, we've laughed
    like no other two people
    could ever laugh —
feeling so far removed from
    the world and not even caring.

Maybe it's the softness in
    your voice,
or the unspoken message
    in your eyes,
or even the simple happiness
    in your laughter
that keeps our friendship
        so special.

Whatever it is . . . it's you.

— Karen S. Clark

85

My Best Friend

A best friend is the most precious
   and special gift
that life has to offer us —
as essential as life itself.
A companionship so absolute that
"stay in touch" rests unspoken,
and is surpassed only by the
   understanding that:
      Tomorrow will never cast its
      rays early enough to shed light
      on my first thoughts of you.
   And the reality that:
      Tomorrow in its entirety could
      never contain all that I wish
      to share with you.
A best friend is someone to whom
   I can turn with the most humble
      idea
and find that by sharing my thought,
   it has transformed into a dream.
A best friend is someone who
   makes happiness,
as tangible and as easy to touch
      as you are close to me.

— Joseph R. Shaver

You know . . .
there is no wealth
but in the feelings we give
    and the feelings we receive.
And friendship
is the greatest gift
we have among us.

— Alexander Balfour

Friends

As we go through this life,
we will make many friends.
Some, we will know for only
   a short while;
others, for a much longer
   time.
Some, we'll always have close
   to us
to share our daily lives;
others, we won't see so often,
yet we'll think of them just
   the same.

Whether they're near or far,
               long or short,
friends are important to have.
Friends are the best there is
   in life.

— Lindsay Newman

My Friend

You have such a
positive outlook on life
Your words are always encouraging
Your face is lit up with excitement
Your actions are so straightforward
Your inner sense helps you achieve
    so much
When people are around you
they seem to absorb your uplifting
    attitude
When I think about you
I can only think
of happiness
and how lucky I am
to know
you

— Susan Polis Schutz

ACKNOWLEDGMENTS

We gratefully acknowledge the permission granted by the following authors, publishers and authors' representatives to reprint poems and excerpts from their publications:

Linda Gatto for "We meet many people," by Linda Gatto. Copyright © Linda Gatto, 1983. All rights reserved. Reprinted by permission.

Paula Finn for "It sounds simple," by Paula Finn. Copyright © Paula Finn, 1983. All rights reserved. Reprinted by permission.

Nancy Kuhlka for "There are people in my life," by Nancy Kuhlka. Copyright © Nancy Kuhlka, 1983. All rights reserved. Reprinted by permission.

Rick Norman for "It feels good" and "Sometimes, I can't believe," by Rick Norman. Copyright © Rick Norman, 1983. All rights reserved. Reprinted by permission.

Nancy Taylor for "Special people," by Nancy Taylor. Copyright © Nancy Taylor, 1983. All rights reserved. Reprinted by permission.

Barbara Lemke for "I am so vulnerable," by Barbara Lemke. Copyright © Barbara Lemke, 1983. All rights reserved. Reprinted by permission.

Paula Morisey for "I didn't ask," by Paula Morisey. Copyright © Paula Morisey, 1983. All rights reserved. Reprinted by permission.

Laura Campbell for "You have a way of bringing," by Laura Campbell. Copyright © Laura Campbell, 1983. All rights reserved. Reprinted by permission.

Rowland R. Hoskins, Jr. for "There is something warm" and "If I could reach," by Rowland R. Hoskins, Jr. Copyright © Rowland R. Hoskins, Jr., 1983. All rights reserved. Reprinted by permission.

Sally E. Blackhall for "My friend . . . ," by Sally E. Blackhall. Copyright © Sally E. Blackhall, 1983. All rights reserved. Reprinted by permission.

Monette for "True Friendship Is Like . . . ," by Monette. Copyright © Monette, 1983. All rights reserved. Reprinted by permission.

Sharon T. Salter for "In this life" and "There are some people," by Sharon T. Salter. Copyright © Sharon T. Salter, 1983. All rights reserved. Reprinted by permission.

Maureen Dixon for "You're becoming very special," by Maureen Dixon. Copyright © Maureen Dixon, 1983. All rights reserved. Reprinted by permission.

Pauline Smith for "The confidence of friendship," by Pauline Smith. Copyright © Pauline Smith, 1983. All rights reserved. Reprinted by permission.

Beth Steward for "To a Friend," by Beth Steward. Copyright © Beth Steward, 1983. All rights reserved. Reprinted by permission.

Bill Lawton for "One of the hundreds of things," by Bill Lawton. Copyright © Bill Lawton, 1983. All rights reserved. Reprinted by permission.